GRAPHIC .

A

Carol Holliday & Jo Browning Wroe

Illustrated by Bubs Renker

First published in 2016 by
Speechmark Publishing Ltd
2nd Floor, 5 Thomas More Square, London E1W 1YW, UK
Tel: +44 (0)845 034 4610 Fax: +44 (0)845 034 4649
www.speechmark.net

Designed and typeset by Moo Creative (Luton)

002-6011/Printed in the United Kingdom by CMP (UK) Ltd

British Library Cataloguing in Publication Data

A catalogue record for this book is available from the British Library

ISBN 978 1 90930 163 4

Ava, come in here, love. We need to talk.
No we don't!
Ava, your best friend is in hospital. She could die. We've got plenty to talk about.
I don't want to talk...
I don't care. We're going to.
I don't want to fight with you, Ava. Have a piece of chocolate cake.
Really?
Jade's at death's door and you want to feed me cake?
Ava, don't push me.
It's you who's pushing me!
EAT IT.
NOOO!

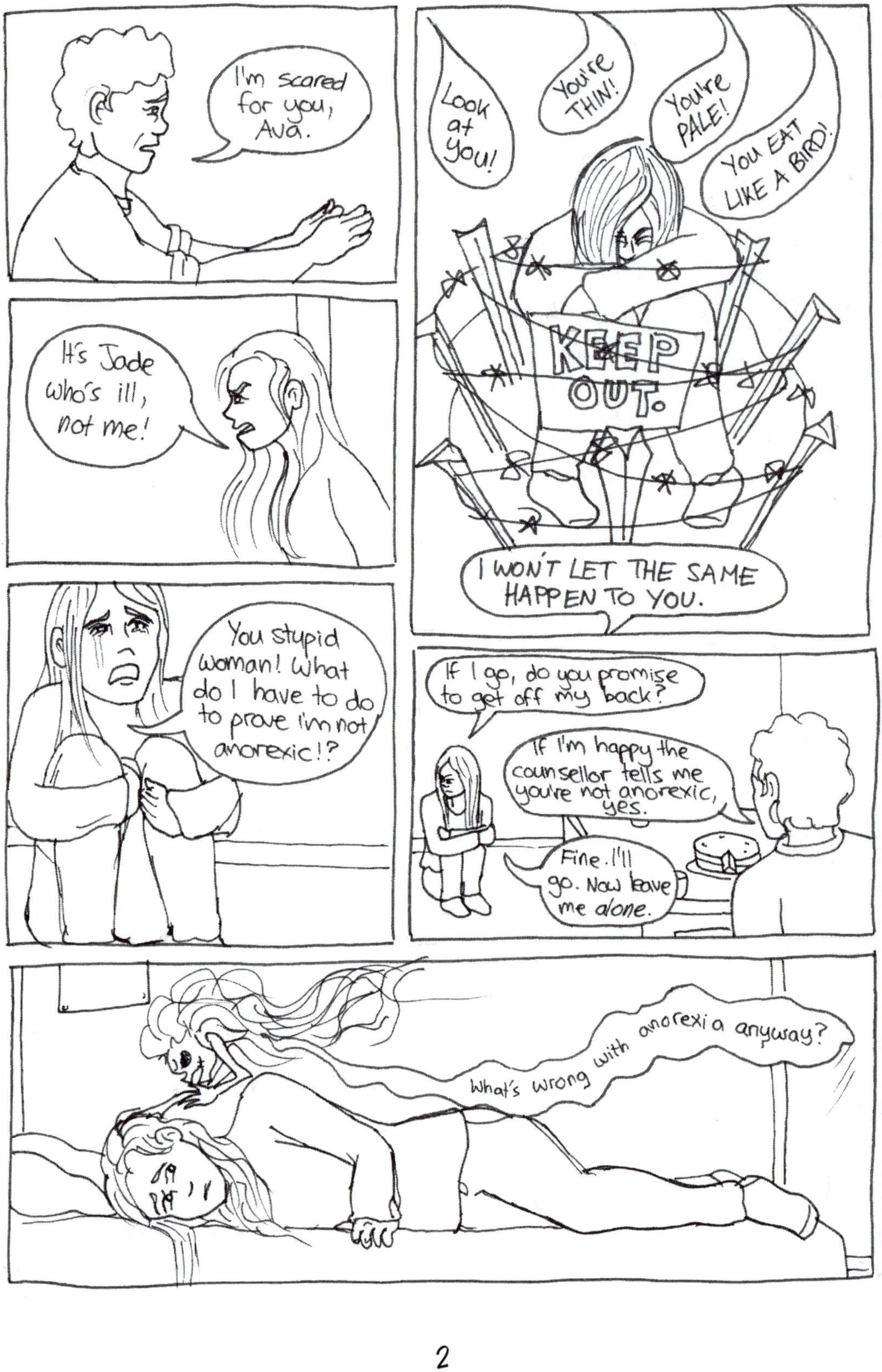
I'm scared for you, Ava.
It's Jade who's ill, not me!
You stupid woman! What do I have to do to prove I'm not anorexic!?
Look at you!
You're THIN!
You're PALE!
You EAT LIKE A BIRD!
KEEP OUT.
I WON'T LET THE SAME HAPPEN TO YOU.
If I go, do you promise to get off my back?
If I'm happy the counsellor tells me you're not anorexic, yes.
Fine. I'll go. Now leave me alone.
What's wrong with anorexia anyway?

This is Jade's best friend. I wonder what's going on for her...
This is stupid. I don't need to be here...
I'm Steph. So today is an initial chat for you to tell me what brings you here. For you to see how I work and for us to decide if we want to work together.
I won't need to come back. You just need to tell my mum I haven't got anorexia.

We're safe in here...
She doesn't want to let me in.
Tell me about your mum.
No! I don't need to! Just tell her I'm not ill!
Why do you think she needs to know that?
She's freaked out about Jade, and won't get off my back.

Maybe you could tell me about Jade.
You know about Jade. Everyone at school knows about Jade.
I'd like to hear what you think about her.
She's beautiful.
She's funny.
She gets me.

It sounds like she's a good friend. It must be tough that she's in hospital.
My mum's convinced I'm ill too. If you just tell her I'm not, it will be okay.
The focus of the work here is on you and your thoughts and feelings. You're the expert on you.
I don't know much about you at the moment. If you choose to work with me, it could be I'll have a conversation with your mum. But not now..
How do you feel hearing this?
That there's no point being here.
It must be frustrating not getting what you want.
What the **hell** am I going to tell mum...

How did you get on with the counsellor?
Okay. She thinks I'm fine. She said it must be tough for me with Jade being in hospital.
What about your eating?
I told you. She said I'm fine.
If you're fine, why haven't you eaten your dinner?
Because I *hate* your food!

Take this - You need to eat.
Thanks mum.
Bitch.
9
Well done! You're in control, not her.
peep!
peep!
peep!

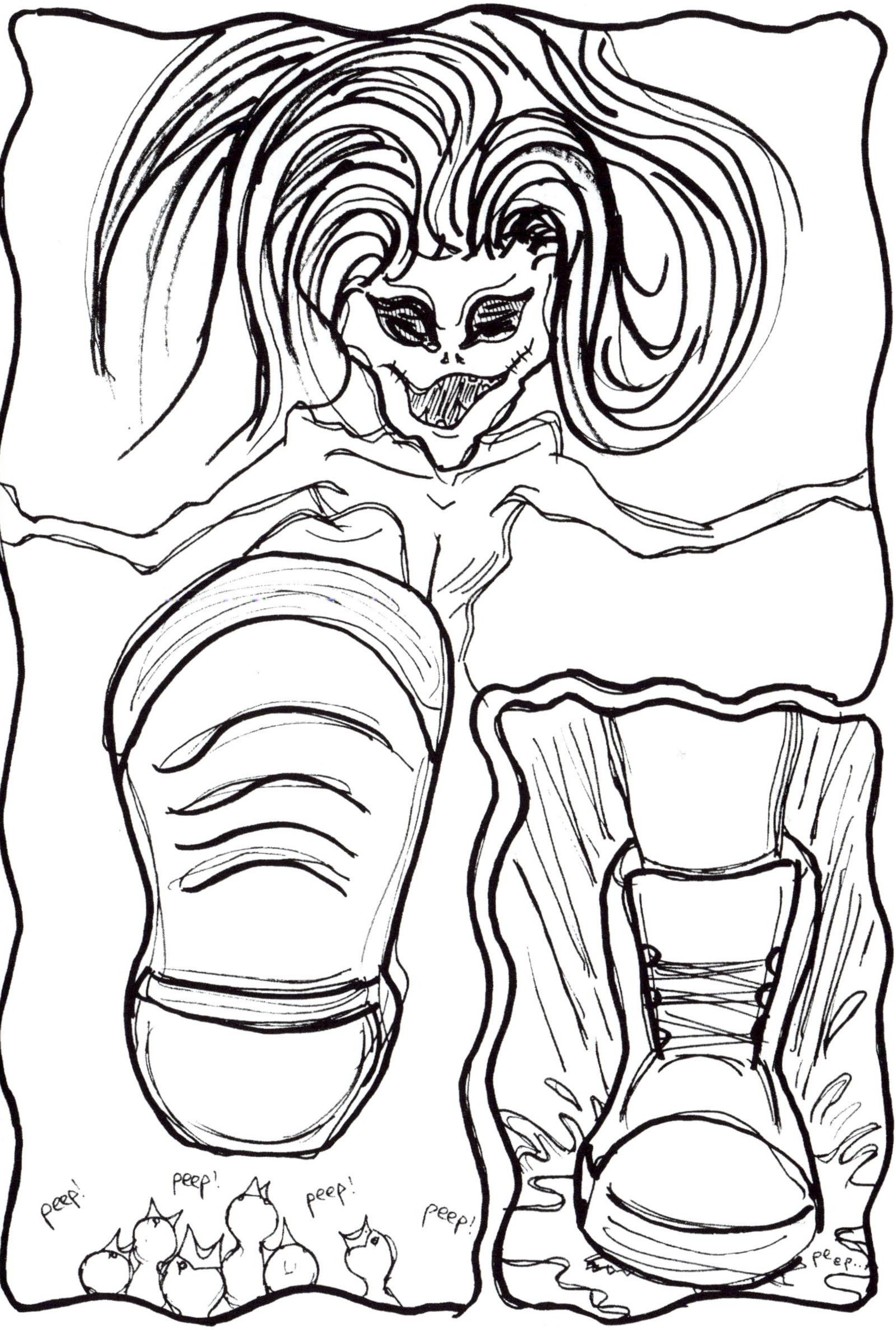
peep!
peep!
peep!
peep!
peep...

I'm not hungry. My mum gave me a massive cooked breakfast.
Ava
We don't need her. We're fine.
peep!
peep!
peep!
peep!
Dear Ava,
It was good to meet you. I hope you will come back next Wednesday and I will hold a place for you at 1:00 pm.
Warm wishes,
Steph

Baking again?
It's coconut and lime. What do you think?
Thanks. Aren't you going to have one?
I've already had one.
Everyone knows about Jade. They were talking about her at work.

Back off! I'm fine
I'm worried about you!
Leave me alone!
Atta girl...
Jade
Hi Jade. Hope you're okay I'm really missing you. I haven't seen you for weeks. Home awful. Mum's on my back all the time. You're the only one who understands me. I'm coming to see you tomorrow!
19:45

Jade hasn't got back to me. But I'm going anyway - she probably hasn't got a signal...
I've come to see Jade Lambert.
I'm sorry but you need to come with Jade's parents.
But I'm her best friend!
Really sorry. We have to stick to the rules.
Ava! What a surprise!
I just went to see Jade. They wouldn't let me in. Can I come with you? I miss her.

That's very nice of you. Jade's really ill. I'll need to talk to her mum. I'll text you later ok?
Thanks. I really want to see her.
...So what do you think?
I think it would be great!
You don't think it would upset Jade?
We said last night she'd lost touch with everyone. This could be just what she needs.
BZZ
BZZ
BZZ
11:05
TODAY
Hi Ava. We'd love for you to come. We'll pick you up at 6.
16:32

...
It's good to see you again. What brings you here?
DON'T LET HER IN!
Sometimes things are difficult to talk about. The work we do here is about feelings, thoughts, and memories. When we get stuck in life, it's to do with feelings that haven't been allowed to be felt or thought about. Here we experience and think about feelings through talk, paint, images in clay, the sand tray, through stories.

You've come back. Part of you wants to let me know what's going on. I suggest you use the miniatures on the shelves to make an image in the sand tray and we'll see what happens.
I want to do this.
Brrmmmmmmmm
You'll see a difference in Jade. She's really poorly. Try not to show it.
She's as bad as my mum...

She looks like a skeleton...
We'll give you some time on your own. We'll be in the lounge.
Why are you here?
I miss you.
This is a mistake.
You should have asked first.
I didn't know friends had to do that.
I don't want this.
Why haven't you been in touch?
I don't want to see anyone.
Maybe it's not all about you. I've been having a shit time.
Leave me alone.

EXIT
You look upset. Shall I take you to your room? What number is it?
Oh my god! She thinks I'm a patient!
I can see that was a painful experience and it hurts for you to tell it.
What was the worst part of that?
Someone thought I was a patient...
What would have made them think that?
They must be stupid! I'm fine!
She's denying how thin she is. I must tread gently.

How do you feel, now you've told me?
Not as bad as I thought it would.
You've let me see a lot about yourself and your feelings?
Shall we agree to work together for the next six weeks?
Okay.

She's really upset today.
I'm going to sit with you.
This silence feels bleak. It's hard to bear.
...
I need to step in.
It seems it's hard to talk today.

Perhaps you can show me what's going on for you.
Tiny. Alone.

I've been dumped by my only friend. I'm so lonely.
That really hurts...
I've never had a friend like her before. We became friends on our French exchange. We stayed with the same family.
Eugh! This meat is so fatty.
I'm going to be sick.
Ca va?
I can't be rude.
C'est tres bien, merci!
Pardon, mais j'ais mal a la... tooth.
I wish I'd thought of that.

Ja i mal a la tooth!
I couldn't remember the French for tooth!
At least you didn't have to eat it!
What are we going to do? I hate the food!
Me too.
Maybe we just ask for tiny portions.
Let's do this...
Look how much weight I've lost!
Me too!
We should make the most of this.
What do you mean?
In two weeks it's the school fashion show. We should audition as models!

Well, now or never. I've never been so thin.
Let's go for it.
We should keep to small portions at home.
Yeah. Until the Show's over.
That was amazing!
I've never felt so good before!
Wow! You look great!
I can see that was a wonderful experience for you.
She thinks being thin gets attention.
This is really important. Time's up for now, but I'll see you next week.
She's hungry for love...

I'm remembering our last session.
You were pathetic last time. Don't let it happen again.
How are you feeling today?
KEEP OUT
Back off. You're as bad as my mum.
Fine.
She's trying to keep me out again.
peep!
peep!
Perhaps you can use the sand tray to show me how you're feeling?
You don't need food. You don't need anything...

Or is there something else you want to do?
I'll just pretend. Anything to keep her off my back.
Sand tray's fine.
Tell me about your image.
This is a bully.
How's the chick feeling?
How do you think?

Frightened?
Hurt?
Upset?
Angry?
Confused?
What's going on in you?
I'm remembering Year 8.

CRASH!
CREAK!
Ava the elephant!
Ava the elephant!
YEAR 8
YEAR 9
YEAR 10
And that's what they called me for 3 years until the fashion show.
How horrid for you... What did you feel?
Everything you said. And shame. And it never went away.
How do you feel now having told me this?
A bit relieved.
You took a risk telling me this. You are very brave. You're doing the work here.
No!

I've been thinking about what a lot you're dealing with...
You think your mum is always getting to you.
You've learned to hate yourself.
You've been badly hurt by being bullied.
You've been affirmed for being thin.
And I've been dumped by my best friend.
All of that has had a big impact on you.
Yes. And I think about food all the time.
Tell me about that.
It's just always there...
It must be hard to concentrate on anything else with all that going on.
But I can't stop! I'm obsessed.
There's part of you that's obsessed and there's a healthy part of you that's working here.
Can you show me that obsessive part of you on the paper?
DONT YOU DARE! I DON'T WANT TO!
But I'm not happy like this...
I'll try.

What shall we call her?
Ana.
I think you need to have a conversation with her.

I don't want to think about food all the time.
But I'm trying to look after you.
I'm not sure I can trust you anymore. I feel so awful.
You have to be thin or people won't love you.
But I'm so hungry all the time.
You mustn't be weak.
Let me tell you something.
In the 1940s a Scientist, Ancel Keys, researched the effect of starvation on a group of fit, healthy young men with no history of depression, anxiety, food or body issues. After months of restricted eating they became obsessed with food. They couldn't concentrate, had low energy and motivation, depression, irritability and body disastisfaction. Even when they had access to food again they were obsessed about eating. Some had episodes of binge eating. The point is, Ava, you are experiencing the response of normal healthy people to food restriction. Starving yourself affects the mind as well as the body... So you're not weak. This would happen to everyone.
It's hard to deal with your feelings through food.
So what do I do?
You're doing it. The way forward is to talk about your feelings, feel your feelings

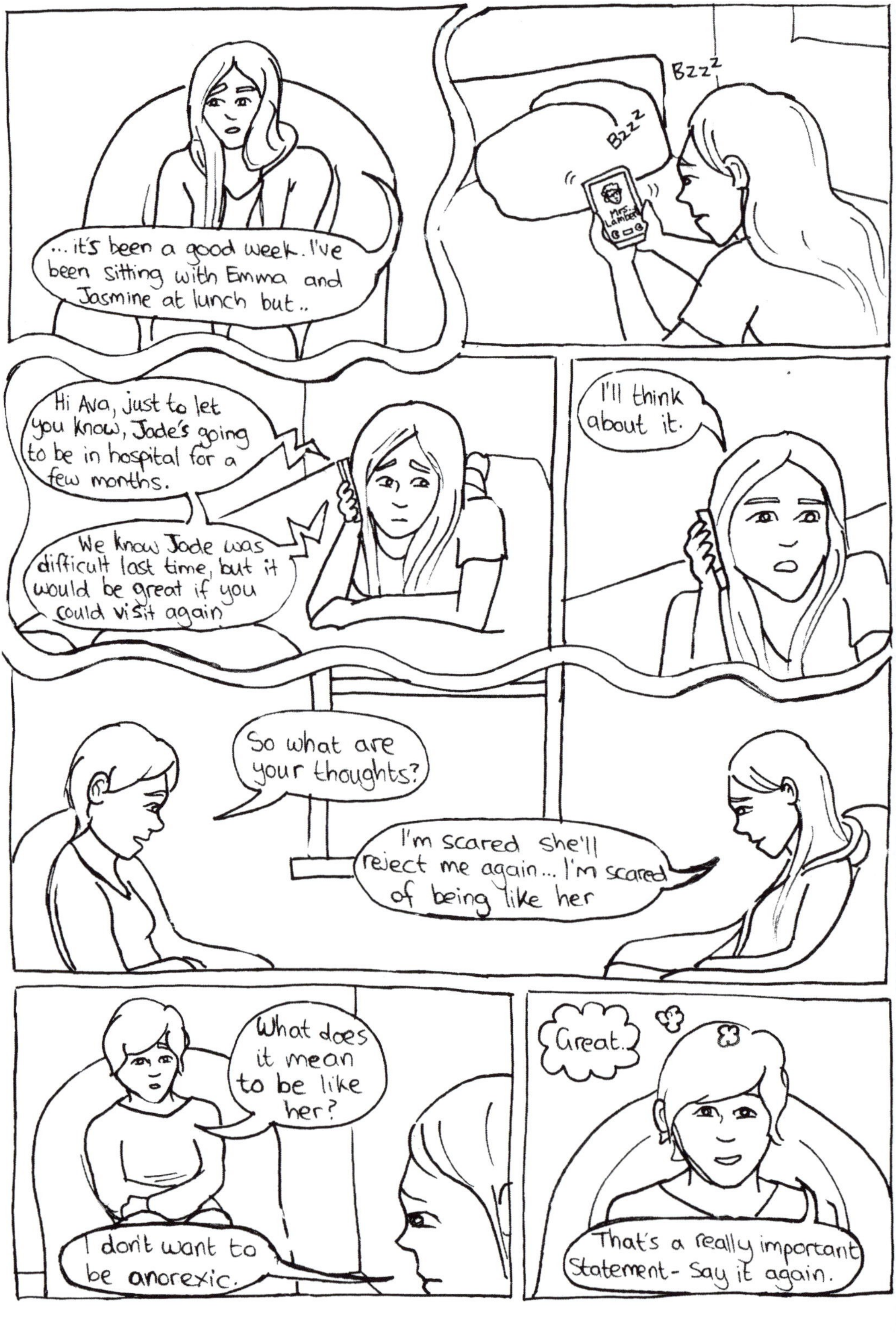
... it's been a good week. I've been sitting with Emma and Jasmine at lunch but..
Bzzz
Bzzz
Mrs. Lambert
Hi Ava, just to let you know, Jade's going to be in hospital for a few months.
We know Jade was difficult last time, but it would be great if you could visit again
I'll think about it.
So what are your thoughts?
I'm scared she'll reject me again... I'm scared of being like her
What does it mean to be like her?
I don't want to be anorexic.
Great.
That's a really important Statement - Say it again.

I don't want to be anorexic.
What if Ana comes back?
You can't unhappen your experiences but you can live well with them.
But what does that mean? How can I stop Ana coming back?
You can't, but when she does, you can manage her.
You can be kind to yourself. You can allow yourself to feel your feelings, you can express them with safe people and think about them. Your feelings are important.
I feel scared of seeing Jade again. What if she sends me away again?
She might.

Bzz
EMMA
Bzz
I'd love to but I'm going to see Jade at the unit.
Hello?
Hi Ava! Me and Jasmine are going to the cinema tonight. Want to come?
Thanks for asking.
I haven't been invited out in ages.
Okay! Maybe next time.
It's good of you to come, Ava. We know Jade isn't easy.
It's okay. She's my best friend.
Hi Jade. Thanks for letting me come.
Mum and dad made me. They think it's good for me.
Don't you want me here?
The thing is, it's hard for me to see you.

KEEP OUT
Maybe it's best to go to the cinema now...
Ok. I won't stay, but I'd like to come again if you want me to.
Hi Emma! I'm free after all. Can I still come?
How was Jade?
Not great. She didn't really want to see me.
oh dear, that must have been hard.
It was. But I get that She's ill. Anyway, I went out with Emma and Jasmine.
Brilliant!
She's right, it was.

... and Jade said it's difficult to see anyone, even me.
How did you feel?
I didn't like it, I felt shut out.
Tell me more about that feeling.
I feel different now.
Tell me more.
I'm not thinking about food as much. I can get on with more things.
And Ana?
I think Ana's different too.
She seems Smaller. Not so bad...
Can we meet this Ana?

Ana is trying to protect you. But stopping you eating and keeping people out wasn't helpful...
Ana has learnt to protect you in better ways.
I can see that now.
Will she stay like that?
When times are tough, she might revert. Your job is to know that and to know old Ana's ways are not good for you. Remember there are better ways.

What's the flavour? Is it cinnamon?
Mixed spice. Like it?
Yeah.
Just enjoy it.
I want to give her a second piece but I should back off.
Doing anything this afternoon?
Shopping with Emma?
Great! Have a good time!
Thanks, mum.
What for?
Being patient with me. I know I can be difficult.
I'm difficult sometimes too. When I worry about you, I can be a bit ferocious.
KEEP OUT.
I'm sorry, Ava.

It's okay. It's been better lately, hasn't it?
I feel as if I can reach you again. I know the problems haven't gone away, but at least we can help each other.